T0009938

America
Second Editions

A Walk in the Tundra

2nd Edition

by Rebecca L. Johnson

with illustrations by Phyllis V. Saroff

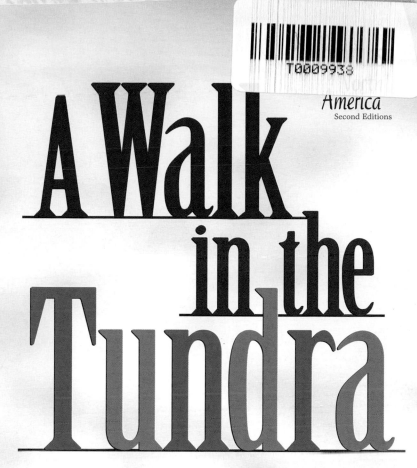

Lerner Publications • Minneapolis

For Adelyn

Text copyright © 2021 by Rebecca L. Johnson
Illustrations copyright © 2021 by Lerner Publishing Group, Inc.
Map on page 8 by Laura Westlund © 2021 by Lerner Publishing Group, Inc.

All rights reserved. International copyright secured. No part of this book may be reproduced, stored in a retrieval system, or transmitted in any form or by any means—electronic, mechanical, photocopying, recording, or otherwise—without the prior written permission of Lerner Publishing Group, Inc., except for the inclusion of brief quotations in an acknowledged review.

Lerner Publications Company
An imprint of Lerner Publishing Group, Inc.
241 First Avenue North
Minneapolis, MN 55401 USA

For reading levels and more information, look up this title at www.lernerbooks.com.

Main body text set in Garth Graphic Std.
Typeface provided by Adobe Systems.

Library of Congress Cataloging-in-Publication Data
Names: Johnson, Rebecca L., author. | Saroff, Phyllis V., illustrator.
Title: A walk in the tundra / by Rebecca L. Johnson ; with illustrations by Phyllis V. Saroff.
Description: 2nd edition. | Minneapolis : Lerner Publications , 2021. | Series: Biomes of North America | Includes bibliographical references and index. | Audience: Ages 8–12 | Audience: Grades 4–6 | Summary: "The tundra is a windy and cold landscape. But the closer you look, the more life you see. Mosses, grasses, and wildflowers grow in the thin soil. Animals from bees to bears depend on the life growing in this chilly habitat"— Provided by publisher.
Identifiers: LCCN 2020033813 (print) | LCCN 2020033814 (ebook) | ISBN 9781728429274 (library binding) | ISBN 9781728429281 (paperback) | ISBN 9781728429298 (ebook)
Subjects: LCSH: Tundra ecology—Juvenile literature. | Tundras—Juvenile literature.
Classification: LCC QH541.5.T8 J65 2021 (print) | LCC QH541.5.T8 (ebook) | DDC 577.5/86—dc23

LC record available at https://lccn.loc.gov/2020033813
LC ebook record available at https://lccn.loc.gov/2020033814

Manufactured in the United States of America
1-49450-49516-8/4/2020

Words
to Know

ALGAE (AL-jee)—tiny, plant-like living things

ARCTIC—the cold region around the North Pole, north of the Arctic Circle

BACTERIA (bak-TEE-ree-uh)—microscopic, one-celled living things found almost everywhere

BIOME (BYE-ohm)—a major community of living things that covers a large area, such as a grassland or a forest

CLIMATE (KLYE-mut)—a region's usual pattern of weather over a long period of time

CYGNETS (SIG-nets)—baby swans

DISGUISE (dis-GIZE)—something that hides a living thing's true identity

EXTINCT—no longer living on Earth

FUNGI (FUHN-gye)—living things such as mushrooms or molds that get their food by breaking down dead plant and animal matter

LICHEN (LYE-ken)—small, crusty living things made up of fungi and algae growing together

PERMAFROST (PUR-muh-frawst)—permanently frozen ground

POLLEN—fine, powdery material made by flowers. Pollen is often yellow.

PREDATORS (PREH-duh-turz)—animals that hunt and eat other animals

PREY (pray)—animals that are hunted and eaten by other animals

SHRUB—a low-growing plant with woody stems and branches

TUNDRA—a cold, treeless plain near the top of the world

Cold wind across the arctic tundra

Overhead, a snowy owl soars through the pale blue sky. Spring sunlight glows on her broad white wings.

Something small and furry moves in the grass. The owl swoops. She catches a lemming in her long, sharp claws. But this food is not for her. The owl has hungry chicks to feed. With the lemming in her beak, she spreads her wings and flies off across the arctic tundra.

In some places on the tundra, rolling hills rise to rugged slopes (above). Other parts of the tundra are almost flat (right).

Tundra. The word sounds like the place. It's lonely, windy, and cold. There isn't a tree in sight, just mile after mile of empty plain. The arctic tundra is so wide and open it seems as if the land could swallow the sky.

Where is the tundra? If you fly south from the North Pole, arctic tundra is the first land you see. It covers the northern parts of all the continents that surround the top of the world. In North America, tundra stretches from the Arctic Ocean south to the middle of Canada.

Biomes of North America

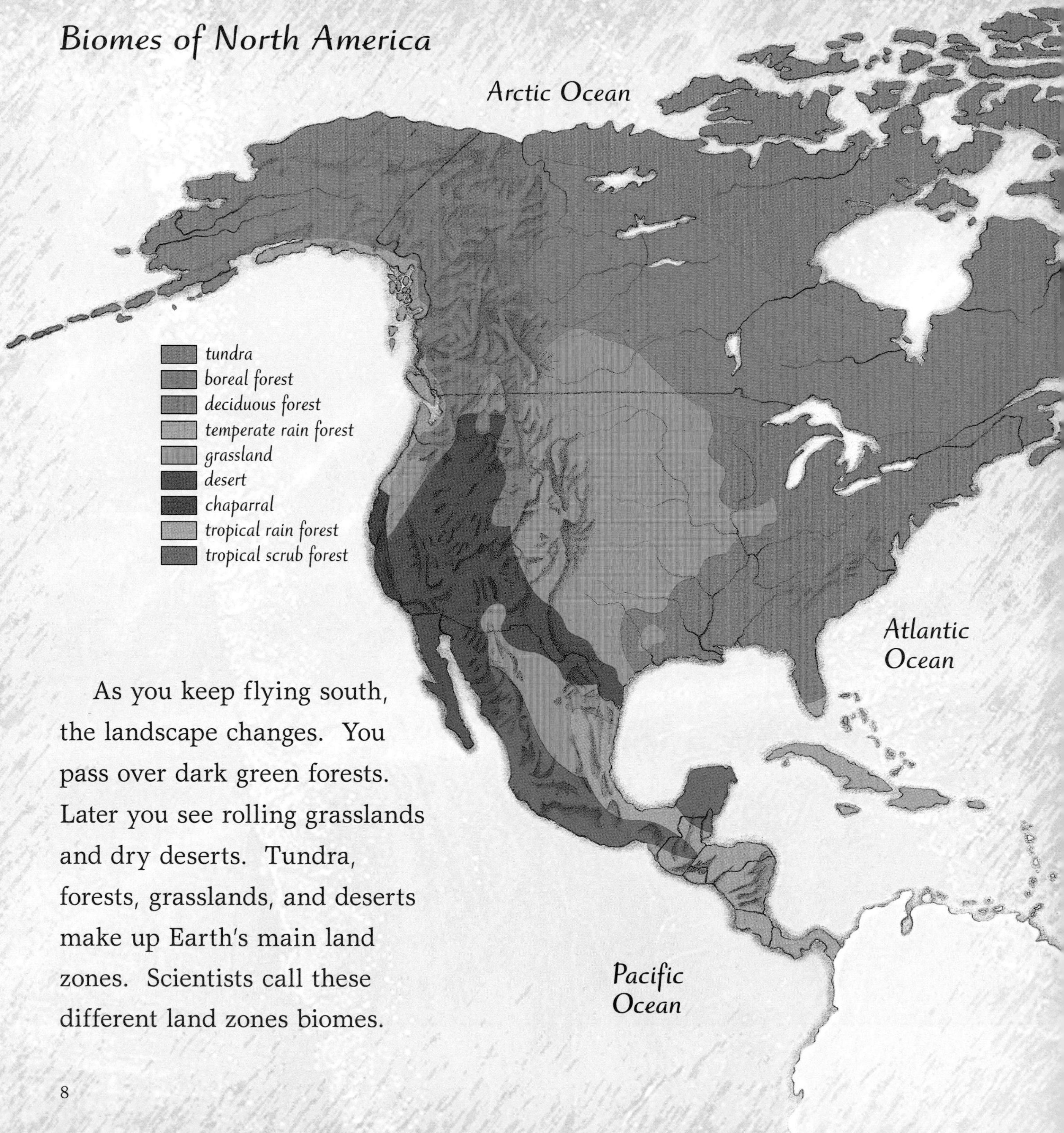

Arctic Ocean

tundra
boreal forest
deciduous forest
temperate rain forest
grassland
desert
chaparral
tropical rain forest
tropical scrub forest

Atlantic Ocean

Pacific Ocean

As you keep flying south, the landscape changes. You pass over dark green forests. Later you see rolling grasslands and dry deserts. Tundra, forests, grasslands, and deserts make up Earth's main land zones. Scientists call these different land zones biomes.

Each biome has a different type of climate. The climate is an area's usual pattern of weather over a long period of time.

Every biome is home to a special group of plants. The plants are well suited to living in that climate and to growing in the soil found there.

Every biome is also home to a special group of animals. In one way or another, the animals depend on the plants to survive. Many of a biome's animals eat plants. Other animals eat the plant-eaters.

Purple saxifrage is well suited to survive the tundra's harsh climate. It is one of the first plants to bloom each spring.

In winter, temperatures drop far below zero on the tundra.

100° F
90°
80°
70°
60°
50°
40°
30°
20°
10°
0°
-10°
-20°
-30°
-40°
-50°
-60°

All the plants and animals in a biome form a community. In that community, every living thing depends on other community members to survive. A biome's climate, soil, plants, and animals are all connected this way.

The arctic tundra has a cold, dry, harsh climate. From September through May, the tundra is locked in winter's icy grip. The ground is frozen as hard as stone. Snow sweeps across the land, driven by howling winds.

Tundra animals, such as these musk oxen, must endure long, bitterly cold winters.

Winter days are short. The nights are very long. In the tundra's far north, the sun doesn't come up at all at midwinter. It is dark both night and day.

The winter sun sets on the snow-covered tundra.

Tundra summers last just three months, from June through August. But summer days on the tundra are long and sunny. The sun shines both day and night. Midnight is nearly as bright as noon.

This photo shows how the sun moves above the horizon, hour by hour, during a summer night at the edge of the Arctic Ocean.

In summer, temperatures may get above 50°F. But frost is still possible in July.

100°F
90°
80°
70°
60°
50°
40°
30°
20°
10°
0°
-10°
-20°
-30°
-40°
-50°
-60°

13

Frozen bodies of extinct animals, such as the woolly mammoth, are sometimes found buried in the permafrost, perfectly preserved.

At the beginning of the summer, sunshine and warmer temperatures melt the snow that winter left behind. But because summer is so short, only the top few inches of soil thaw out. Deeper down, the ground never thaws. This ground that is always frozen is called permafrost.

Spring sunlight
begins to melt the
snow (left).
Where the tundra
meets the sea, you
can see permafrost
underneath the top
layers of soil (right).

Tender shoots push up through damp tundra soil in spring (left). On high ground (below), white tufts of cotton grass sway in the cool summer breeze. Shallow pools cover the tundra in lower areas.

It is early summer. The breeze is cool, but the sun is warm. Let's take a walk on the tundra. We can see what life is like in this biome near the top of the world.

The surface of the tundra is getting soggy as it thaws. Feel how squishy the ground is beneath your feet? Because of the permafrost, water can't soak into the ground.

16

Convstant freezing and melting make tundra ground lumpy and cracked and hard to walk on.

The water collects in low spots. There, it forms shallow lakes and ponds. Parts of the tundra are dotted with these pools of water for most of the summer. Yet it rarely rains. So on higher ground, the soil can get very dry.

Most tundra plants have shallow roots. Roots can't grow into permafrost.

Poke your finger into the soil at your feet. It is cold, gritty, and damp. Just a few inches down, it's frozen solid. Worms, fungi, and bacteria break down dead plant and animal matter that collects on the ground. They turn it into soil. The soil feeds the plants and helps them to grow. But because the tundra soil is always quite cold, fungi and bacteria

Low-growing tundra plants bloom in a rainbow of colors during the short summer.

here work very, very slowly. So the soil is thin and poor. It contains only a little bit of what tundra plants need to grow well.

As you walk along, notice how short the plants are. Few grow more than knee-high. Tundra plants hug the ground to escape the fierce winds. They form a dense mat that covers the land like a thick carpet.

Clumps of soft moss grow along the banks of a stream (above). White anemone (bottom right) and tiny campion flowers (top right) bloom just inches above the ground.

Bend down for a closer look. You'll see mosses, grasses, and wildflowers. Run your fingers over a patch of moss. Its dark green surface is velvety soft.

Many different kinds of plants grow on the tundra. They are all crowded together. Most have small leaves that are tough and leathery. Small leaves stand up to cold and wind better than large leaves do. Some leaves are covered with soft little hairs. These tiny hairs trap water. They help keep tundra plants from drying out.

A covering of tiny hairs helps keep the arctic poppy's leaves and stems from drying out.

The leaves of a least willow glow in the sun. Least willows are related to willow trees found in other biomes, but grow only a few inches to a foot high.

21

Bees carry pollen from flower to flower. With pollen, flowers make seeds.

Summers go by so quickly on the tundra that the plants must hurry to grow. As soon as the snow begins to melt at the end of winter, green shoots pop up. They sprout from seeds or roots that survive the long, cold months underground. As flowers begin to bloom, the tundra explodes with color. The plants must flower and make seeds before winter returns.

Small shrubs grow on the tundra, too. They don't die back to the ground at the end of summer, like flowers do. Instead, their woody stems grow a little bit each year. So don't be fooled by their small size. Many of these shrubs are older than your parents are.

An arctic ground squirrel feeds on the buds of a shrub (above left). Blooming tundra plants attract bees and other insects with bright, showy flowers (far left).

Lichens come in all shapes and sizes (left).
Colorful lichens grow everywhere on the tundra—
even on bare rock (below).

Lichens grow on the ground and on rocks. Some look like splashes and smears of orange, yellow, and black paint. Lichens are very tough. They can survive in the coldest, driest places, where nothing else can grow.

Green plants and colorful lichens are food for many tundra animals. Listen. Hear that rustling in the grass? It's a lemming. A lemming looks like

Mother lemmings give birth to their babies in underground burrows.

a big short-tailed mouse. It's about the size of your hand. Summer is a busy time for lemmings. They scurry from place to place, looking for grasses and seeds to eat.

The lemmings are also busy starting new families. Some summers, mother lemmings give birth to many babies. When that happens, the lemming population gets very, very large. Already this year, lemmings seem to be *everywhere* on the tundra.

A collared lemming looks for more plants to eat.

If you look carefully, you might see some of the other animals that live on the arctic tundra year-round. An arctic hare crouches behind that clump of grass. You can just see the tips of its ears. It is hiding from an arctic fox. Arctic foxes are predators. Predators hunt and eat other animals.

An arctic hare, in its grayish brown summer coat, blends in with its background (above). But a hare whose white winter coat has not yet changed is easier for predators to see (right).

A fox's fur has two layers. Soft, fluffy underfur keeps in heat. Long, thick guard hairs block the wind.

Both arctic hares and arctic foxes have thick, fluffy coats of fur to keep them warm in the winter. These wonderful fur coats change color during the year. In summer, arctic hares and foxes have grayish brown fur that matches the rocks and soil. In winter, their coats become white, which blends in with the snow. Summer or winter, these animals wear a perfect disguise.

Arctic foxes, still in winter white, watch intently as something moves in the grass nearby.

A ptarmigan's large outer feathers keep out wind and snow. Its inner down feathers are fluffy and trap heat.

In her summer coat of spotted feathers, this ptarmigan blends into her surroundings. When she stands still, she is almost invisible.

The ptarmigan has a white coat in winter, too. But its coat is made of feathers. When summer comes, a ptarmigan grows feathers that are spotted brown and gray. A ptarmigan is resting among some plants. You might not even notice her until she moves out into the open to look for seeds to eat. But when she does, she will be careful. She is being watched from the sky.

Snowy owls soar over the tundra, summer and winter. These great white birds are fierce predators. They catch and eat ptarmigans, arctic hares, and even arctic foxes. But a snowy owl's favorite food is lemmings.

A snowy owl parent brings a lemming to its fluffy chicks.

A pack of arctic wolves hunts together on the tundra.

Lemmings, hares, foxes, and ptarmigans all have to watch for even bigger predators. Arctic wolves roam the tundra, too. They live in family groups called packs.

And huge, powerful polar bears live along the tundra's edges, where land meets icy sea. Polar bears spend most of their time near the water,

hunting seals. A polar bear is one animal you do *not* want to meet while walking across the tundra. Polar bears can run surprisingly fast and will eat anything they can catch.

A polar bear sniffs the breeze on a sunny summer day.

A young musk ox stays close to its mother while the herd walks and eats plants.

Let's climb to the top of a low hill for a better view. Far off in the distance, you can see some of the strangest-looking tundra residents. Musk oxen are great, shaggy beasts with long hair that almost reaches the ground. They live in herds, like cattle. Their pointed, curved horns are good weapons against polar bears and wolves.

When danger threatens, musk oxen stand shoulder to shoulder in a line, facing their enemy. They lower their sharp horns, snort loudly, and stomp their mighty hooves. If they're surrounded by a pack of arctic wolves, musk oxen will form a tight circle with their heads and horns pointing out. Their babies stay in the middle where it's safe.

When musk oxen are surrounded by wolves, they make a circle with their horns pointing out.

Grazing as he goes, a musk ox bull wades through tundra plants. His pointed horns are very sharp.

Caribou have big hooves that keep them from sinking into snow or mushy wet ground.

Every year, when the snow begins to melt, other animals arrive. These summer visitors move up from the south to spend June, July, and August on the tundra. Caribou come in huge herds to eat the

A hungry caribou calf nurses while its mother watches for danger (above). *A herd of caribou splash through a shallow river as they move across the tundra* (left).

grasses and lichens. They also come to give birth to their calves. Do you see the caribou herd in the distance? Thousands and thousands of caribou move slowly over the treeless plain.

A nest of eggs is well hidden.

With wings flapping, greater white-fronted geese descend on a shallow tundra lake. They will build their nests out of grasses.

Most of the summer visitors are birds. Watch them winging their way across the sky. They come by the millions to build nests, lay eggs, and raise their chicks on the tundra.

Tundra swans honk loudly as they fly overhead. Crowds of geese and ducks and loons paddle across shallow lakes and build nests along the banks. A sandhill crane strides about on long legs. She's on the lookout for foxes and owls. Those predators would like to eat the crane's eggs, lying hidden in the grass.

Smaller birds, like redpolls and white-crowned sparrows, flit from perch to perch. They never fly far from their secret nests. Their hungry, downy chicks huddle in the nests, waiting for food.

And what do most tundra chicks eat? Insects! Shallow pools and damp ground are perfect places for all sorts of insects to lay their eggs. Clouds of newly hatched mosquitoes rise from lakes and ponds. Blackflies and gnats fill the air. Do you hear them buzzing and humming? Can you feel them crawling on your skin?

Mosquitoes hatch in pools of water.

Hungry mosquitoes swarm over a loon as she sits on the eggs in her nest.

37

The mosquitoes and biting flies can be ferocious. But the swarms of insects are wonderful food for hungry baby birds. Mother and father birds fly through the air or walk in the grass, snapping up flies and bugs. Back at their nests, they stuff their catch into their chicks' gaping mouths. Then they quickly fly off again to gather the next meal.

A tundra swan swims with its three fluffy cygnets (left). Newly hatched Lapland longspur chicks wait in their nest for food (top). Nearby, their father has just caught a mouthful of juicy insects (above).

The birds on the tundra work day and night to bring food to their chicks. They are racing against time. Summer will soon be over. Young birds must grow quickly. They must be ready to fly before the cold and darkness of winter return.

Other tundra babies are also growing fast under the midnight sun. Fox pups wrestle with each other. They try to catch lemmings in the grass. Caribou calves scamper and jump. Young musk oxen still stick close to their mothers. But they are getting stronger and bigger each day. Everywhere you look, the tundra is full of light and color and life.

Arctic fox pups play hard and grow quickly.

Seeds of most tundra plants are small enough to be scattered by the wind. The arctic poppy has very tiny seeds.

As winter approaches, the leaves of tundra plants, like the least willow, turn from green to gold, bronze, and scarlet (left). Ripe, ruby-red lingonberries (below) are eaten by arctic foxes and polar bears.

But it won't last long. Already, berries are getting ripe, and seeds are falling to the ground. In just a few weeks, the green color of the tundra plants disappears. The plants put on their fall colors—fiery reds, deep purples, and dark golds.

Near the end of August, the summer birds fly south to warmer places. Flocks of ducks and geese look like giant Vs scrawled across the sky.

The herds of caribou move south, too. They slowly tramp across the faded tundra, nibbling lichens as they go. The caribou spend the winter in the great forests south of the tundra. There, they are sheltered from the wind and can find enough food to eat.

As summer ends, caribou begin their journey south.

A ptarmigan's feathery "snowshoes" keep it from sinking into the snow.

The sun gets lower in the sky each day. Stinging cold winds blow down from the North Pole, bringing frost and then snow. The blanket of snow protects seeds and roots from the bitter cold.

By September, all the summer animals are gone. Only the hardy animals remain.

Thick coats of feathers and fur change from brown to white. The ptarmigan even grows feathers between its toes. Like snowshoes, these fluffy feathers help the ptarmigan walk on top of the snow.

In their white winter coats, ptarmigans puff their feathers against the cold wind.

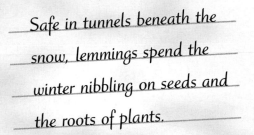

Safe in tunnels beneath the snow, lemmings spend the winter nibbling on seeds and the roots of plants.

A mother polar bear and her cub brave bitter cold and blowing snow during the long winter.

Some tundra animals sleep the winter away in underground burrows. Lemmings stay awake. They scurry through their tunnels beneath the snow and snack on seeds and roots.

But many other animals have no place to hide from winter's fury. The musk oxen, foxes, and polar bears depend on thick layers of fat and fur to survive the winter. They brave darkness, subzero temperatures, and howling winds for nearly nine months.

But eventually, the long, dark winter on the arctic tundra will end. After what seems like forever, the sun will return to glow again on the snowy owl's wings. And the tundra will be bursting with life once more.

An arctic fox uses its fluffy tail to keep its nose and feet warm.

A musk ox's fur and fat protect it from the freezing air of winter.

Tundra in Danger

The tundra is in trouble. A major threat is human activities that release greenhouse gases, such as burning fuels to produce electricity. As greenhouse gases build up in the atmosphere, they trap heat rising from the planet's surface. Earth's temperature is increasing, and climates are changing.

Climate change is making the tundra warmer, both in summer and in winter. In some places, summers are so warm that the permafrost is melting.

Climate change is also making the tundra drier, leading to more fires. Huge wildfires are common. Some burn for many months. When tundra plants burn, caribou and other animals struggle to find enough food.

You can fight climate change by reducing greenhouse gases. Walk or ride a bike instead of taking a motor vehicle. Help your family use less energy by turning off lights when no one is in a room. Slowing climate change protects the tundra's unique inhabitants, including lemmings, musk oxen, and polar bears.

for further
Information
about the Tundra

Cocca, Lisa Colozza. *Tundra Animals*. Vero Beach, FL: Rourke, 2020.

Kids Do Ecology—Tundra
http://kids.nceas.ucsb.edu/biomes/tundra.html

Krajnik, Elizabeth. *Changing Tundra Environments*. New York: PowerKids Press, 2020.

Markle, Sandra. *Mosquitoes: An Augmented Reality Experience*. Minneapolis: Lerner Publications, 2021.

Markle, Sandra. *Snowy Owl Invasion! Tracking an Unusual Migration*. Minneapolis: Millbrook Press, 2018.

NASA Climate Kids—What Is Climate Change?
https://climatekids.nasa.gov/climate-change-meaning/

San Diego Zoo Animals & Plants—Tundra
https://animals.sandiegozoo.org/habitats/tundra

World Wildlife Fund—Polar Bear
https://www.worldwildlife.org/species/polar-bear

Photo Acknowledgments

Image credits: Nature Picture Library/Alamy Stock Photo, pp. 4-5; inEthos Design/Shutterstock.com, p. 6; Chris Howey/Shutterstock.com, p. 7; Ingrid Maasik/Shutterstock.com, p. 9; Frank Fichtmüller/Getty Images, p. 10; Vadim_Nefedov/Getty Images, p. 11; Design Pics Inc/Alamy Stock Photo, pp. 12-13, 22, 35, 37, 38 (top right); troutnut/Getty Images, p. 14; peace portal photo/Alamy Stock Photo, p. 15; Sanamyan/Alamy Stock Photo, p. 16; Josef Hanus/Shutterstock.com, pp. 16-17; Sergio Ponomarev/Shutterstock.com, pp. 18-19; Robert Szymanski/Shutterstock.com, p. 20 (left); John Ruberry/Shutterstock.com, p. 20 (top right); Nick Pecker/Shutterstock.com, p. 20 (bottom right); Biosphoto/Alamy Stock Photo, p. 21; Michelle Holihan/Alamy Stock Photo, p. 23; Hector Ruiz Villar/Shutterstock.com, p. 24 (left); Jupiterimages/Getty Images, p. 24; Leonid Eremeychuk/Getty Images, p. 25; Sophia Granchinho/Shutterstock.com, p. 26 (left); Johnny Giese/Shutterstock.com, p. 26 (right); Jim Cumming/Shutterstock.com, p. 27; Ian William Hromada/Shutterstock.com, p. 28; Arco Images GmbH/Alamy Stock Photo, p. 29; All Canada Photos/Alamy Stock Photo, p. 30; chbaum/Shutterstock.com, p. 31; Mark Newman/The Image Bank/Getty Images, pp. 32, 34-35; Judd Patterson/Getty Images, p. 33; Steven J. Kazlowski/Alamy Stock Photo, p. 36; Mick Durham FRPS/Alamy Stock Photo, p. 38 (middle right); Andy Wilcock/Shutterstock.com, p. 38 (left); Joe McDonald/Shutterstock.com, p. 39; Vadim Nefedoff/Shutterstock.com, pp. 40-41; Pi-Lens/Shutterstock.com, p. 41; Mint Images/Art Wolfe/Getty Images, p. 42; OLGA ALEXANDROVA/Shutterstock.com, p. 43; outdoorsman/Shutterstock.com, p. 44; Dgwildlife/Getty Images, p. 45.

Front cover: Janet Griffin/Shutterstock.com, Ian William Hromada/Shutterstock.com, CherylRamalho/Shutterstock.com, Paul Souders/Getty Images.
Back cover: Melchakov/Shutterstock.com.

Index

Numbers in **bold** refer to photos and drawings